Essential Blues Bass Grooves

An Essential Study of Blues Grooves for the Bass

By Frank De Rose & David Barrett

SCHOOL OF THE BLUES®

School of the Blues Lesson Series

Online Audio www.melbay.com/21065BCDEB

Audio Contents

1 Introduction
2 Tuning
3 Shuffle: Key of E
4 Slow Blues: Key of G
5 Bo Diddley Beat
6 Rock Beat: Key of G
7 Shuffle: Key of G
8 Shuffle: Key of G
9 Shuffle: Key of G
10 Slow Blues: Key of G
11 Stroll
12 Rock Beat: Key of D
13 Rhumba: Key of C
14 Slow Blues: Key of Gm
15 Rock Beat: Key of Am
16 Shuffle: Key of E
17 Shuffle: Key of A
18 Rock Beat: Key of A
19 Slow Blues: Key of F
20 Shuffle: Key of C
21 Slow Blues: Key of G
22 Two-Beat: Key of D
23 Shuffle: Key of G
24 Two-Beat: Key of A
25 Boogie
26 Two-Beat: Key of E
27 Rock Beat: Key of E
28 Rock Beat: Key of G
29 Shuffle: Key of G
30 Rock Beat: Key of D
31 Shuffle: Key of G
32 Slow Blues: Key of G
33 Swamp Beat
34 Slow Blues: Key of B-flat
35 Billy Boy Arnold Beat
36 Shuffle: Key of D
37 Rock Beat: Key of F
38 Shuffle: Key of A
39 Shuffle: Key of G
40 Slow Blues: Key of G
41 Shuffle: Key of E
42 Backwards Shuffle
43 Slow Blues: Key of F
44 Rock Beat: Key of C
45 Rhumba: Key of G
46 Rhumba: Key of A
47 Stroll
48 Slow Blues: Key of G
49 Thanks

MEL BAY®

1 2 3 4 5 6 7 8 9 0

Table of Contents

Audio Track Navigation

Audio Track Navigation by Groove, Key & Page

Shuffles

Rock Beats

Two Beats

Rhumbas

Slow Blues

Other Grooves

About the Author

Frank De Rose, a prominent fixture in the San Francisco Bay Area Blues scene, brings over four decades of experience to the School of the Blues Lesson Series. Throughout the years he has been a band member with the area's top Blues band leaders and performers including Gary Smith, Tommy Castro, Mark Hummel, Kenny "Blue" Ray, John Garcia, Mike Schermer, Sid Morris and many more. Through these connections, Frank has provided his skills to a long list of national touring Blues performers including Snooky Pryor, Otis Rush, Johnny Heartsman, Nick Gravenites, Andy Just, Chris Cain, Rusty Zinn, Junior Watson, Jackie Payne, Larry Davis, Mississippi Johnny Waters, Luther Tucker, Johnny Adams, Curtis Salgado and many others.

Frank's comprehensive instructional method focuses on providing a solid understanding of the bass player's role in Blues music and a deep study of the music's culture and traditions. He then takes this core of understanding and builds upon it to guide and mold his students into the role of a modern-day Blues musician. His students routinely play and participate in local bands and jam sessions. And when listening to his students, it is unmistakably evident that he is very successful at passing on his passion and knowledge to the next generation of Blues bass musicians.

About the School of the Blues Lesson Series

School of the Blues is a school dedicated to the study of Blues and all the styles it influenced. Founded in 2002 by educator David Barrett, the school thrives today as the center of Blues education in the San Jose/San Francisco California Bay Area.

The instructors at the school and this lesson series have on average twenty years teaching and performing experience. All of the instructors were hand-picked to teach at the school for their playing skills, knowledge of their instrument and ability to teach all skill levels of private and group instruction. We are all dedicated to our craft and receive huge pleasure playing an active role in our students' musical and personal development as well-rounded musicians.

This series is a continuation of this love for the music and its education. David Barrett is the administrator and coauthor of all the books. Many meetings took place with all of the instructors to shape the outline of the books and to make sure that the experience and knowledge of the instructors was contained within each book.

A cornerstone to the School of the Blues instruction approach is showing a student how to apply what they learn. Purchasing *Blues Bass Play-Along Trax* (21064M) is highly recommended to provide you with extended jam tracks to practice with. This series is also designed for students of other instruments to play together. If you have friends that play guitar, harmonica, keyboard or drums, tell them about this series so that you can grow together. There's nothing more fun than making music with other people.

We all wish you the best of luck in your studies. For more information about this series or to contact us, please visit www.schooloftheblues.com.

About This Method

Welcome and thank you for purchasing Essential Blues Bass Grooves, part of the *School of the Blues Lesson Series*. This book and audio contain 46 of the most common Blues grooves every bass player needs to know. The material is presented as a synthesis of the many songs I have listened to, learned and played over the past forty years, and not as an exact representation of any specific song.

Each groove is written in standard and tab notation and has a track number indicator to help you locate the example on the companion audio. The tracks are sparsely recorded with only the bass, drums and guitar, which allows you to focus on the inner workings of the groove. There are no vocals or solos to get in the way. I will play the bass on the first chorus (8 or 12 bars) and then drop out so that you can continue to play the groove with the drums and guitar. All of the tracks start at the beginning of the form (the **I** chord). Consequently, the starting chord is also the key of the song. Rather than just straight 12 Bar Blues, these grooves can be played over many other chord progressions and song structures, such as 8, 16 and 24 Bar Blues, AABA (chorus and bridge) songs and ballad style songs.

I have listed a song title or two for each groove. That means that if this song was called at a recording session, a gig or a jam session, then this is the style of groove that I would play. I strongly recommend that you research these songs and the artists that have recorded them. This task is a lot easier since the advent of online music stores and music databases. Browse through and sample all of them. Purchase the ones you like and make a practice playlist of all the original songs that work with these grooves. What you will find is that in each of the songs, the rhythm section has played the groove a little differently. Sometimes the difference will be subtle, sometimes dramatic.

Finally, in addition to learning the notes of each bass groove, you should become very familiar with the sound of the drum patterns. There are 44 unique drum patterns on the audio and it would be well worth the effort to spend some time studying how the drums and bass fit together. Also, if you are playing in a band or if you jam with a regular group, share this book and audio with the drummer. This coordinated study by you and the drummer will help you to avoid the common Blues band problem of having all of the songs in your setlist sound the same.

Be sure to tell your other band members and friends about the *School of the Blues Lesson Series*. In addition to Bass and Drums, We have books and Play-Along Trax for Guitar, Harmonica and Keyboard.

Now let's get started learning these 46 Essential Blues Bass Grooves.

3 This is a Shuffle, similar to the songs "Baby What You Want Me To Do" and "You Don't Have To Go" performed by Jimmy Reed.

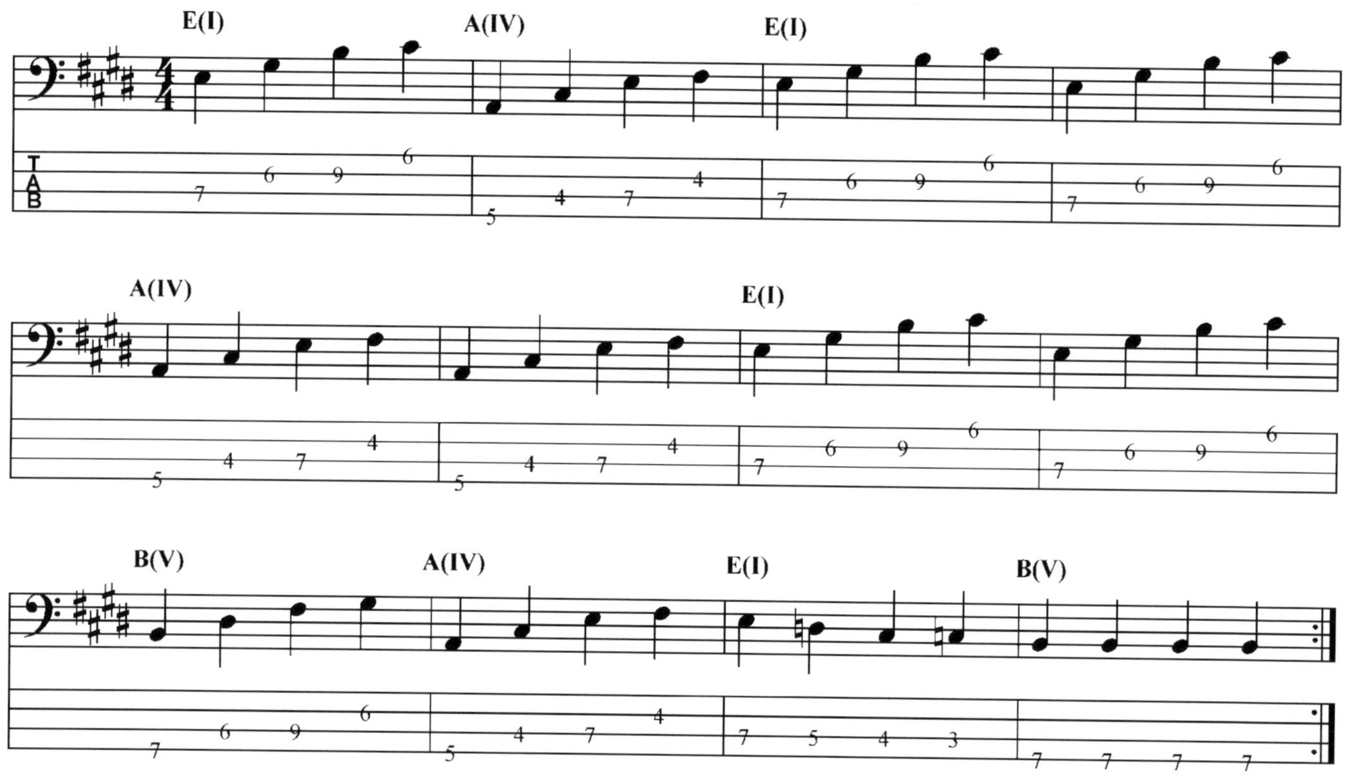

4 This is a Slow Blues, similar to the songs "Blues After Hours" and "T-Bone Blues" performed by T-Bone Walker, as well as "Mean Old World" performed by Little Walter.

5 This is a Bo Diddley beat, similar to the songs "Mona" performed by Bo Diddley and "Not Fade Away" performed by the Rolling Stones.

6 This is a Rock Beat, similar to the songs "Born in Chicago" performed by Paul Butterfield and "Three Hundred Pounds of Joy" performed by Howlin' Wolf.

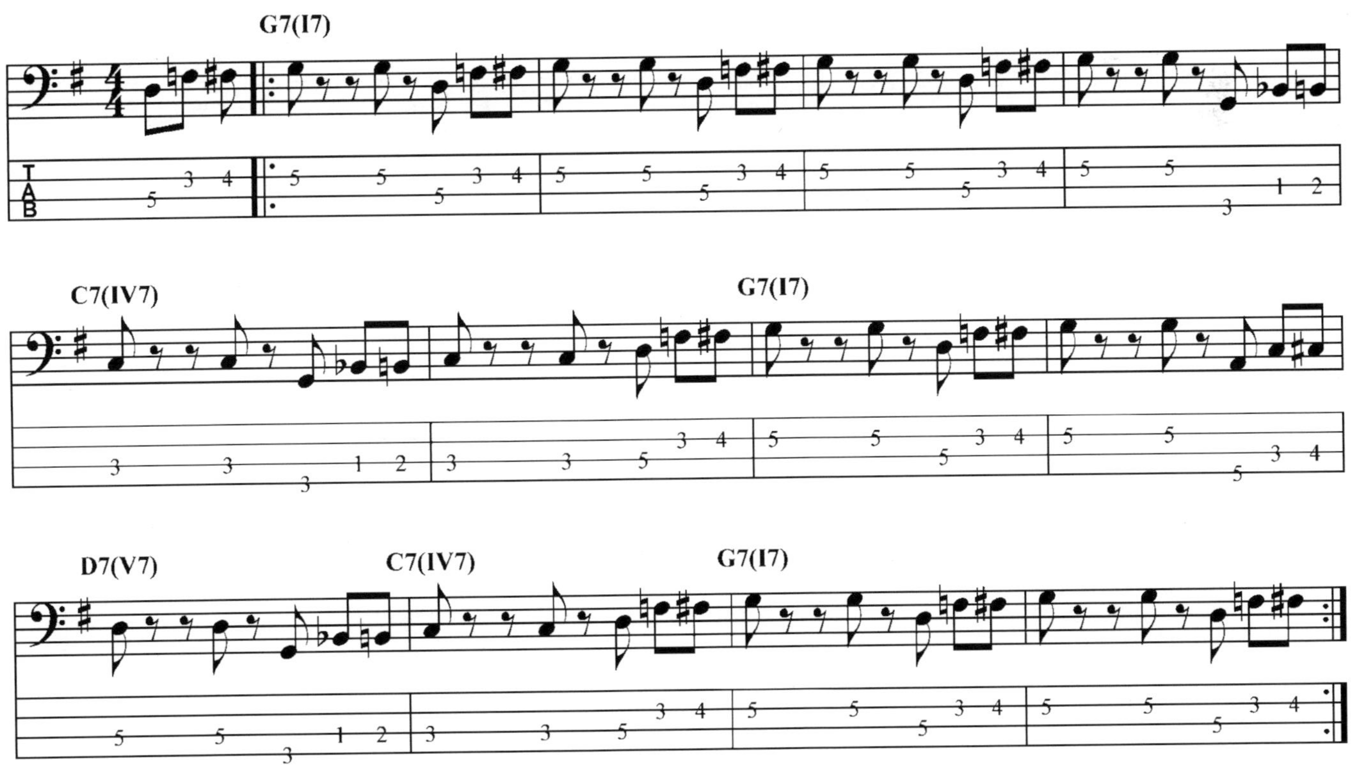

7 This is a Shuffle, similar to the songs "Side Tracked" and "Tore Down" performed by Freddie King, as well as "Everything's Gonna Be Alright" performed by Little Walter.

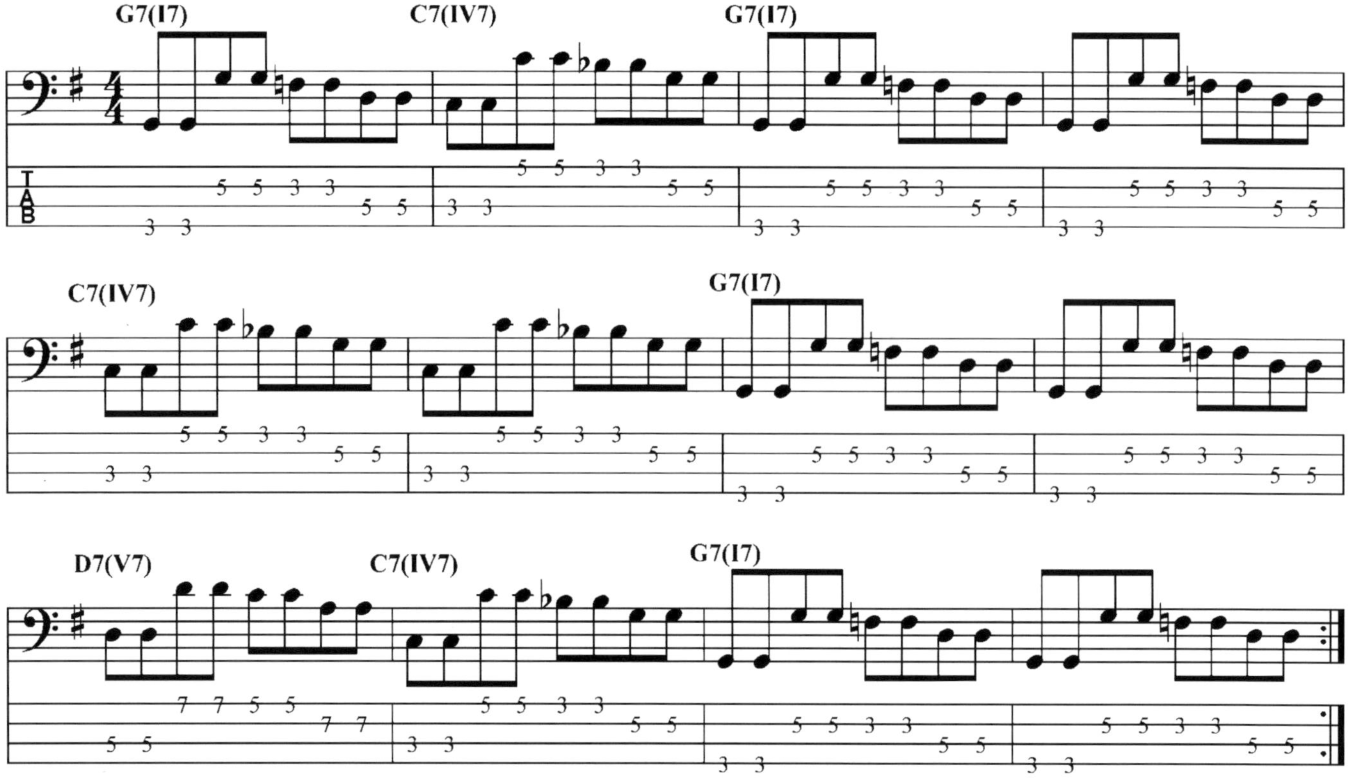

8 This is a Shuffle, similar to the songs "Chicken Shack" performed by Jimmy Smith and "Mudcat" performed by Muddy Waters.

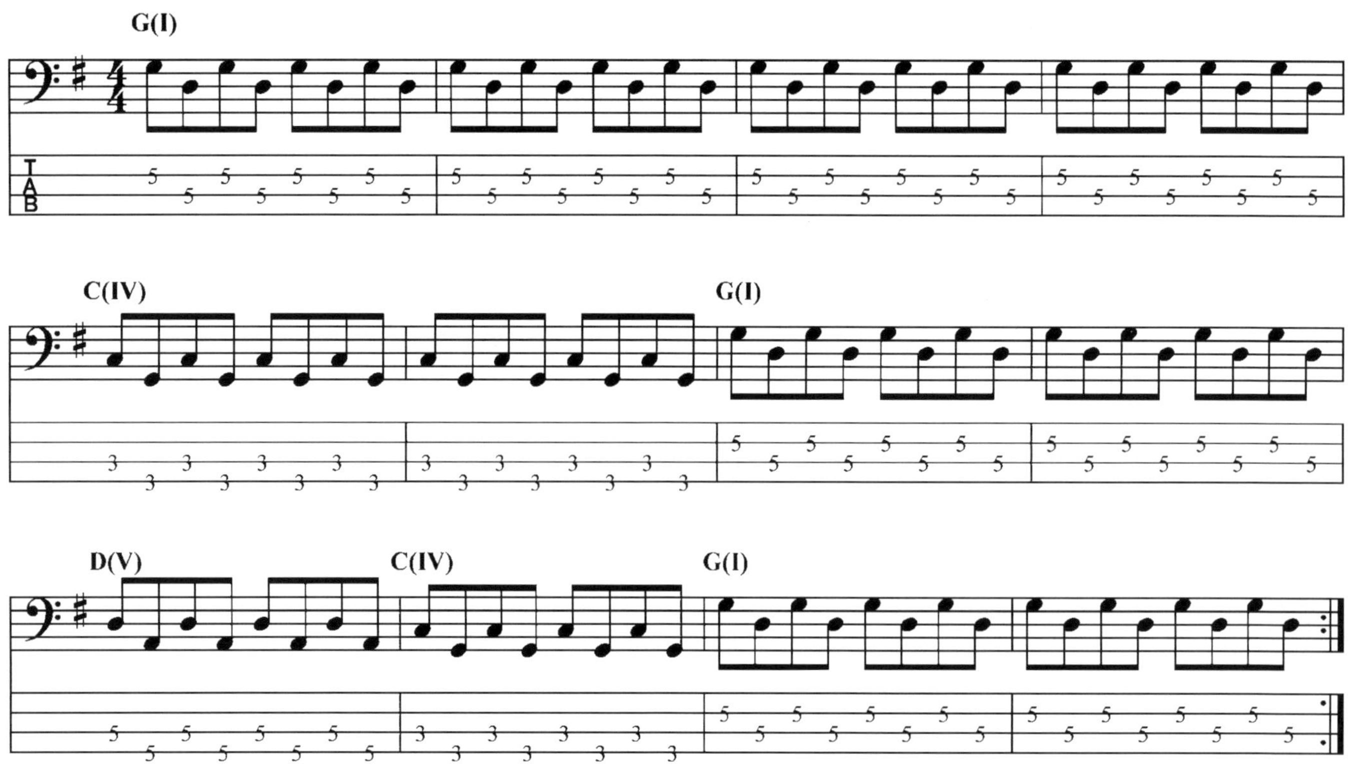

9 This is a Shuffle, similar to the songs “Crap Shoot” performed by James Harman and “I Feel That Old Feeling Coming On” performed by Tommy Castro.

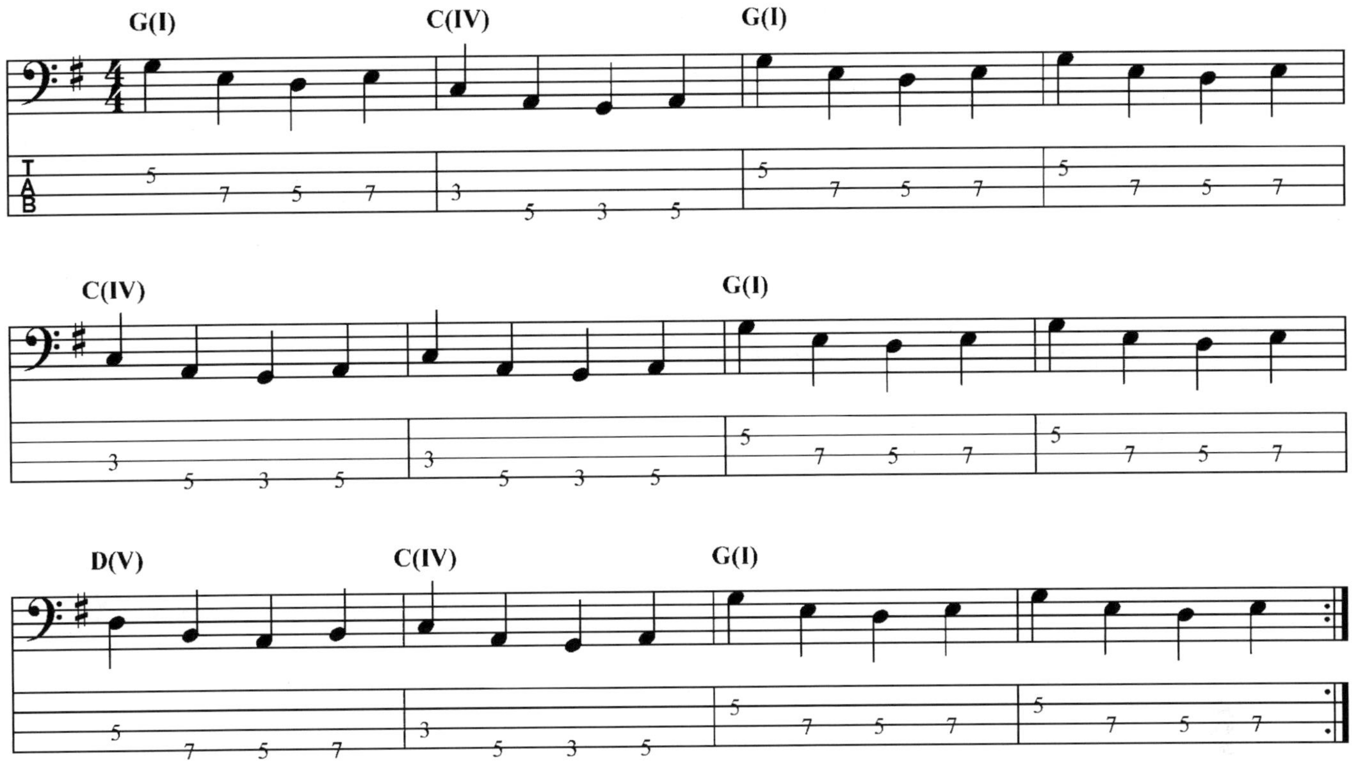

10 This is a 12/8 Slow Blues, similar to the songs “Driving Wheel” by Junior Parker and “Down on Bending Knees” performed by Johnny Copeland.

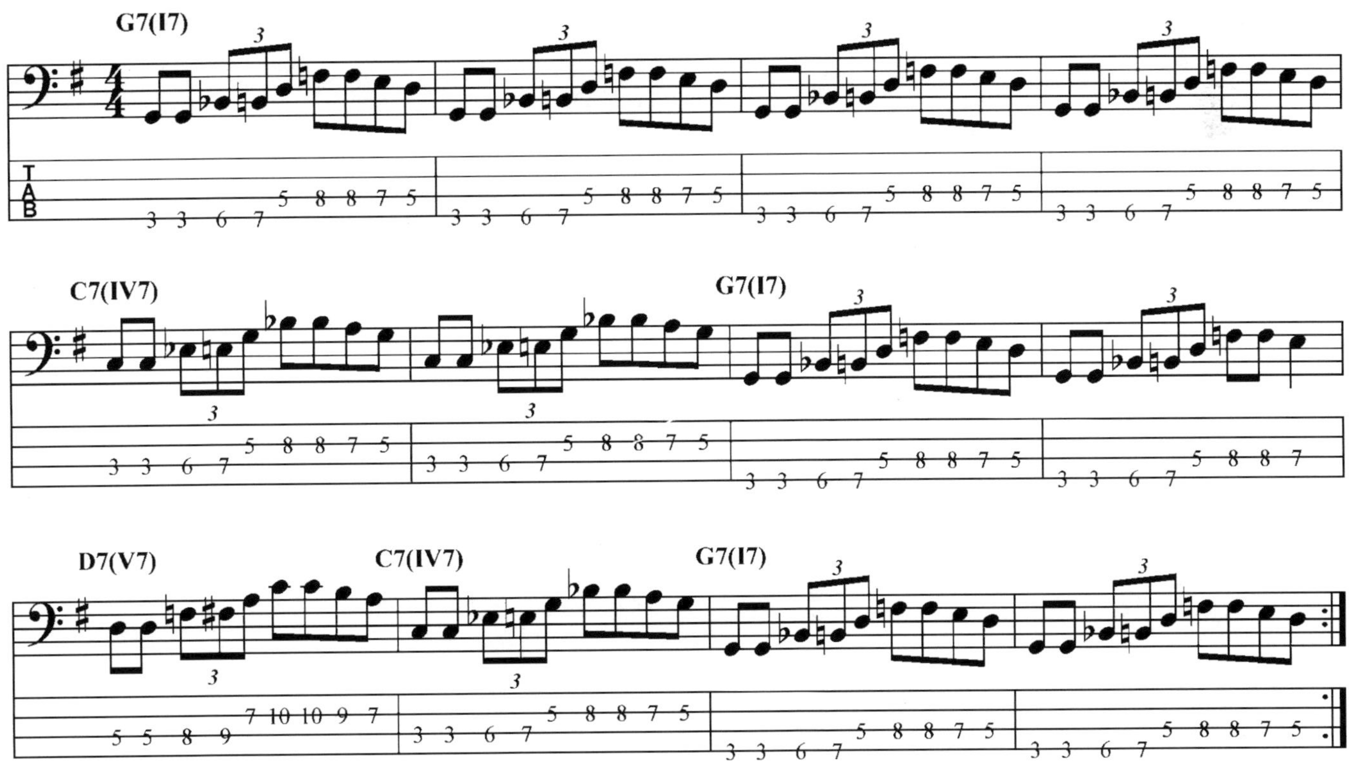

11 This is a Stroll, similar to the songs "Every Time" performed by T-Bone Walker and "Ain't That A Shame" performed by Fats Domino.

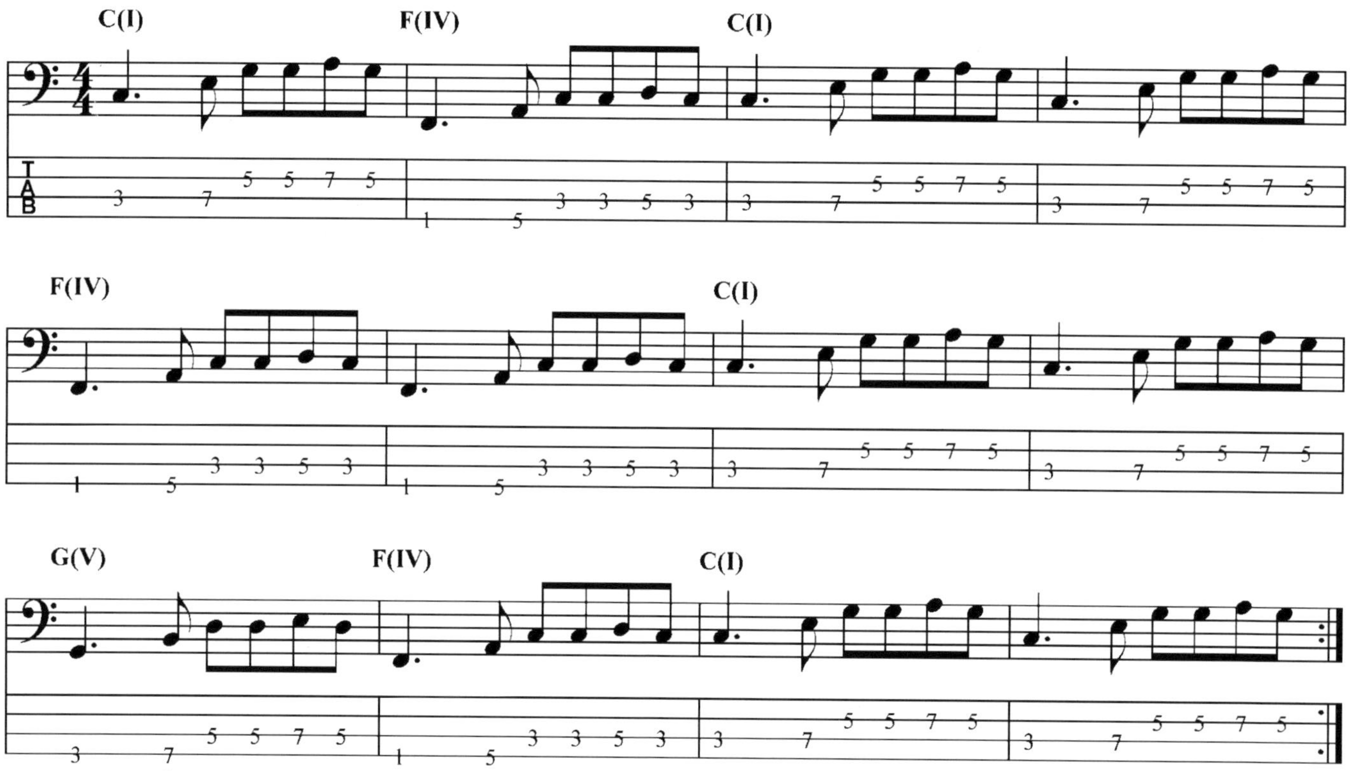

12 This is a Rock Beat, similar to the song "Going Down" performed by Freddie King.

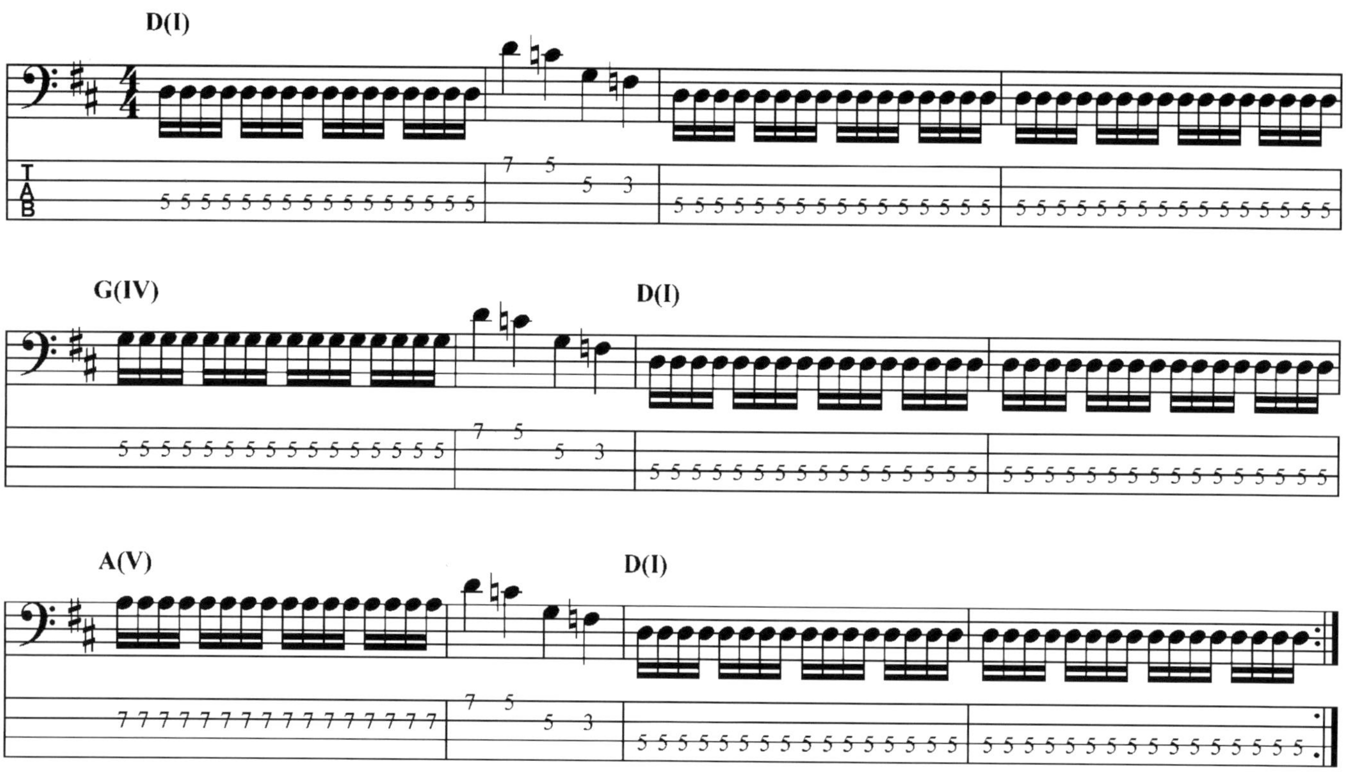

13 This is a Rhumba, similar to the song "Hard Way" performed by T-Bone Walker.

14 This is a Slow Blues, similar to the songs "Help Me" performed by Rice Miller (Sonny Boy Williamson II), "Green Onions" performed by Booker T. & the MG's and "Strange Woman" performed by Muddy Waters.

15 This is a Rock Beat, similar to the songs "Highway 59" performed by the School of the Blues All-Star Band, "All Your Love (I Miss Loving)" performed by Otis Rush and "Black Magic Woman" performed by Santana.

16 This is a Shuffle, similar to the songs "Juke" and "Backtrack" performed by Little Walter, as well as "Hunch Rhythm" performed by Kim Wilson.

17 This is a Shuffle with a swing feel, similar to the songs "T-Bone Shuffle" performed by T-Bone Walker and "Kidney Stew" performed by Eddie "Cleanhead" Vinson.

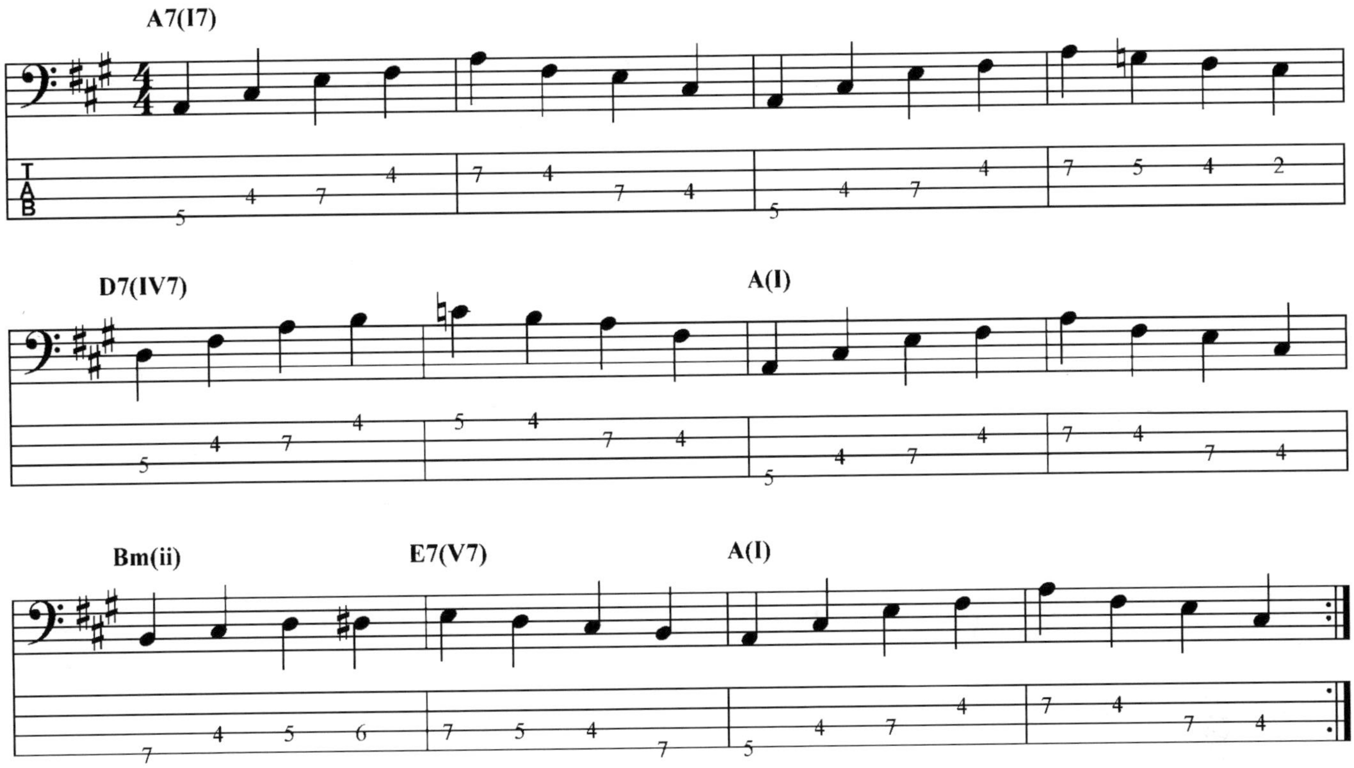

18 This is a Rock Beat, similar to the songs "Killing Floor" performed by Howlin' Wolf and "Pretty Girls" performed by John Garcia.

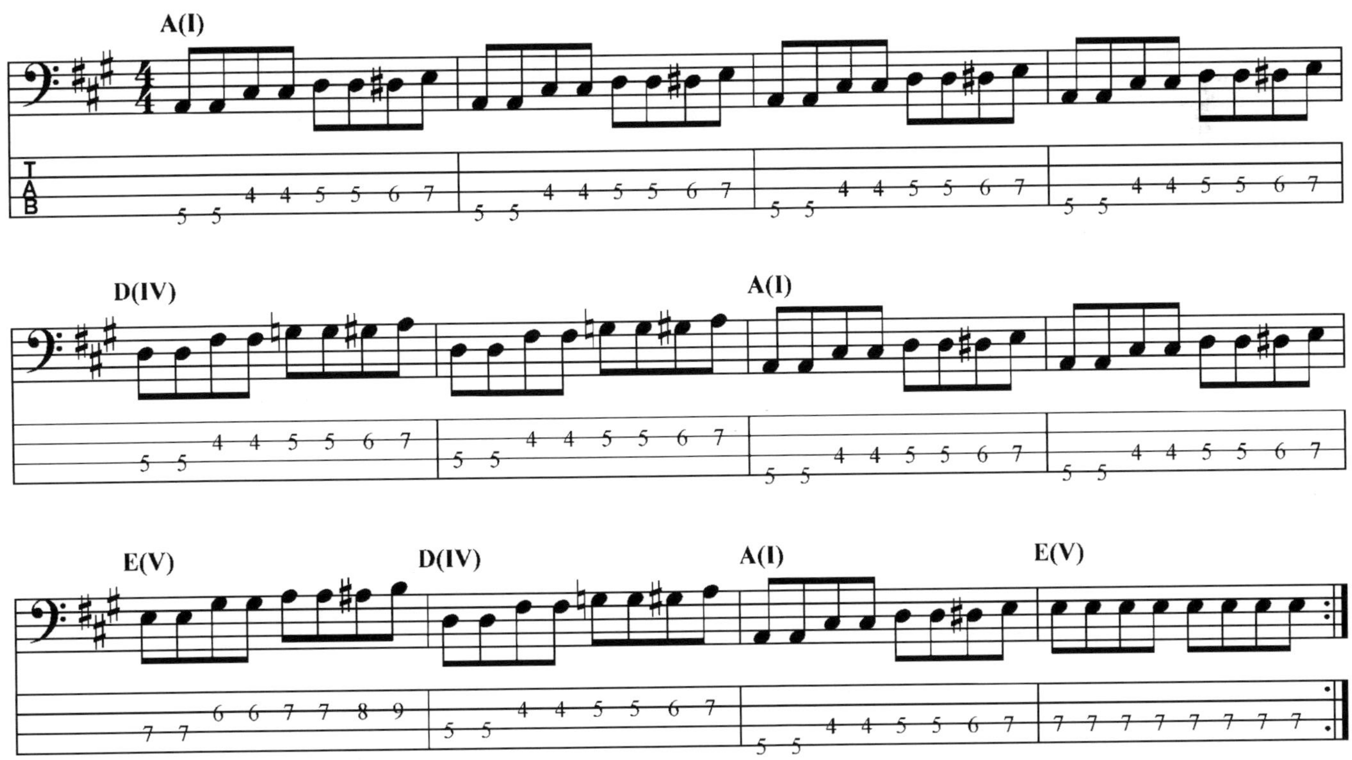

19 This is a Slow Blues, similar to the songs "Last Night" and "Quarter to Twelve" performed by Little Walter.

20 This is a Shuffle, similar to the songs "Left Overs" performed by Albert Collins and the solo section of "Work Song" performed by Paul Butterfield.

21 This is a Slow Blues, similar to the songs "Long Distance Call," "Country Boy" and "What Is That She Got" performed by Muddy Waters.

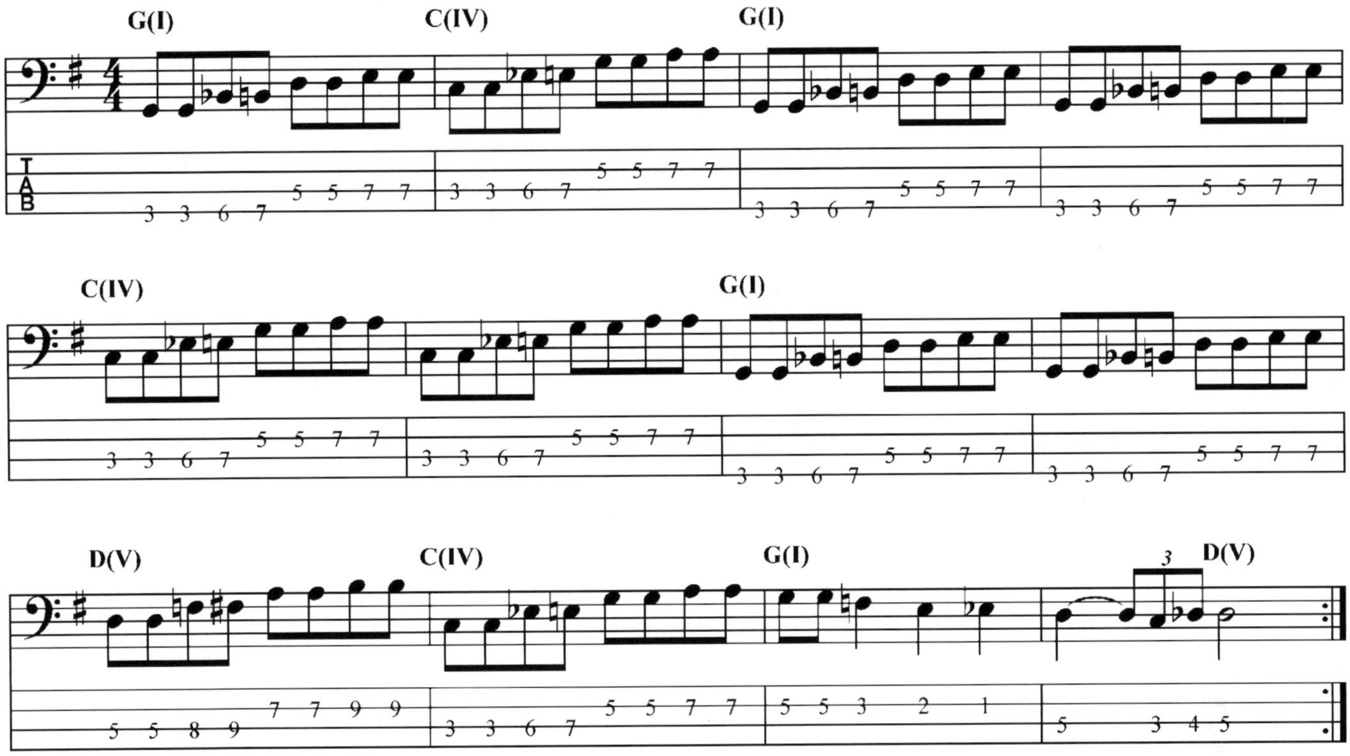

22 This is a Two Beat, similar to the songs "Messaround" performed by Ray Charles and "Shakin' The Shack" performed by Mitch Woods.

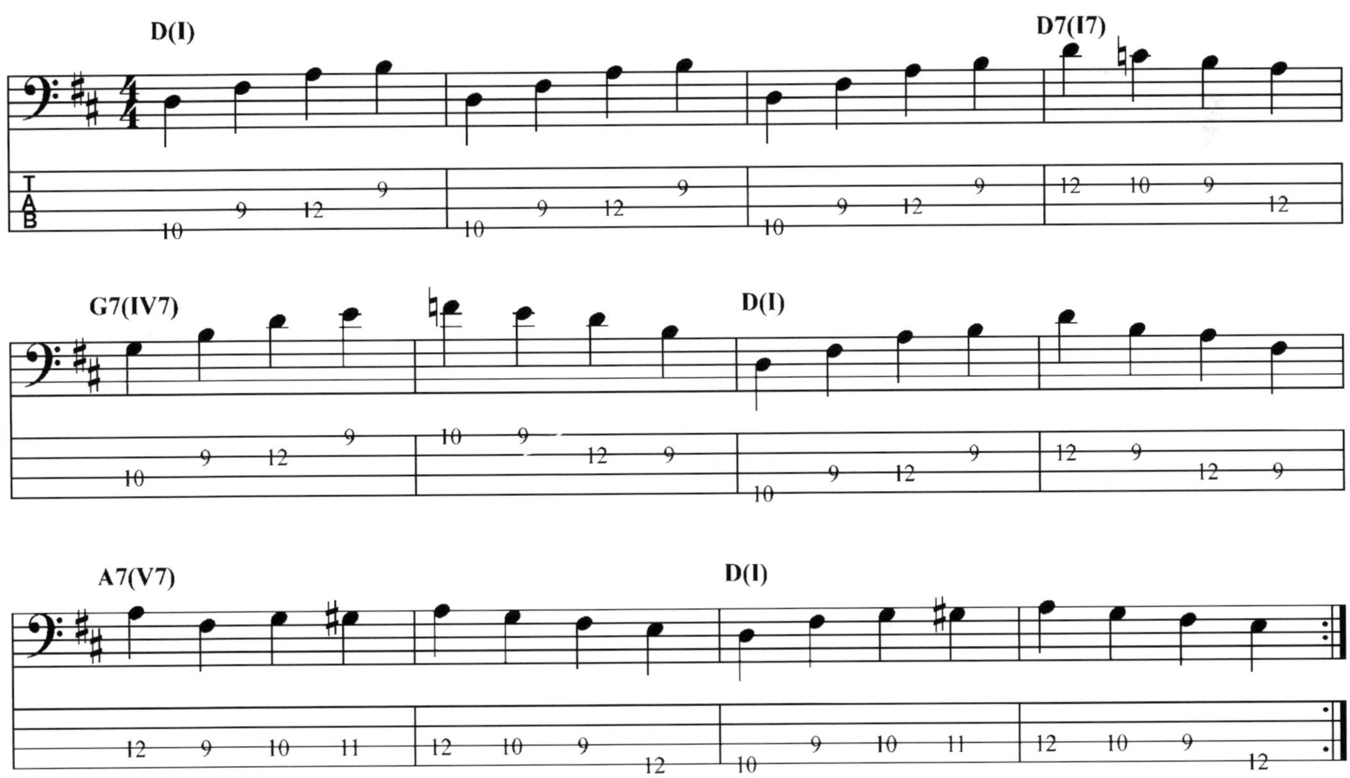

23 This is a Slow Stop-Time Shuffle, similar to the songs "Manish Boy" performed by Muddy Waters and "I'm A Man" performed by Bo Diddley.

24 This is a Two-Beat, similar to the songs "Mellow Down Easy" performed by Little Walter and "Sharp Harp" performed by George "Harmonica" Smith.

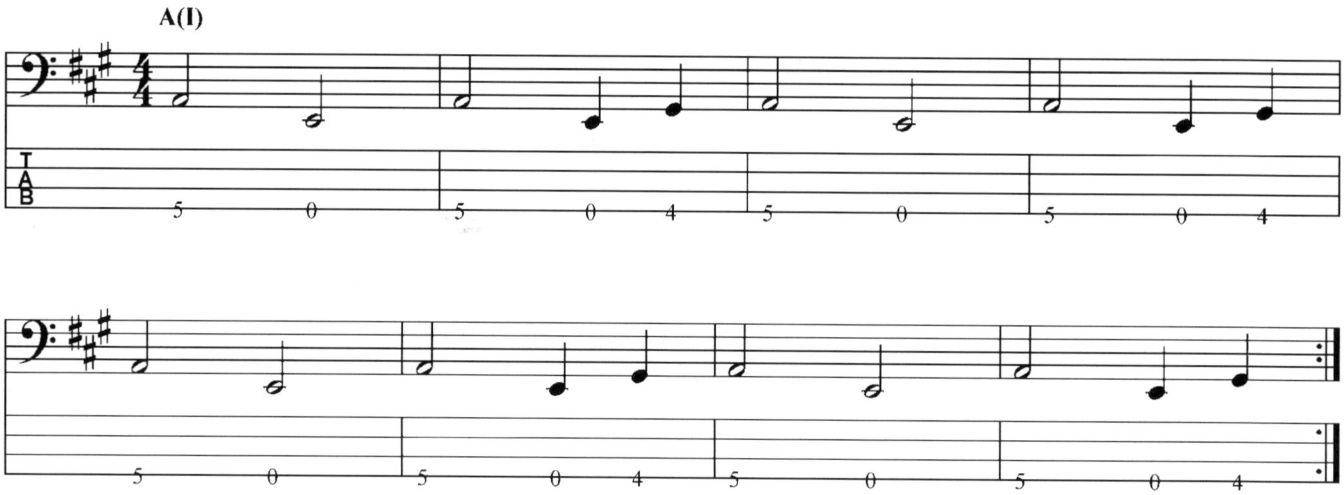

25 This is a Boogie, similar to the songs "Boogie Chillin'" performed by John Lee Hooker, "La Grange" performed by ZZ Top and "Boogie Thing" performed by James Cotton.

26 This is a Two-Beat, similar to the songs "Got My Mojo Working" performed by Muddy Waters and "Please" performed by Mark Hummel.

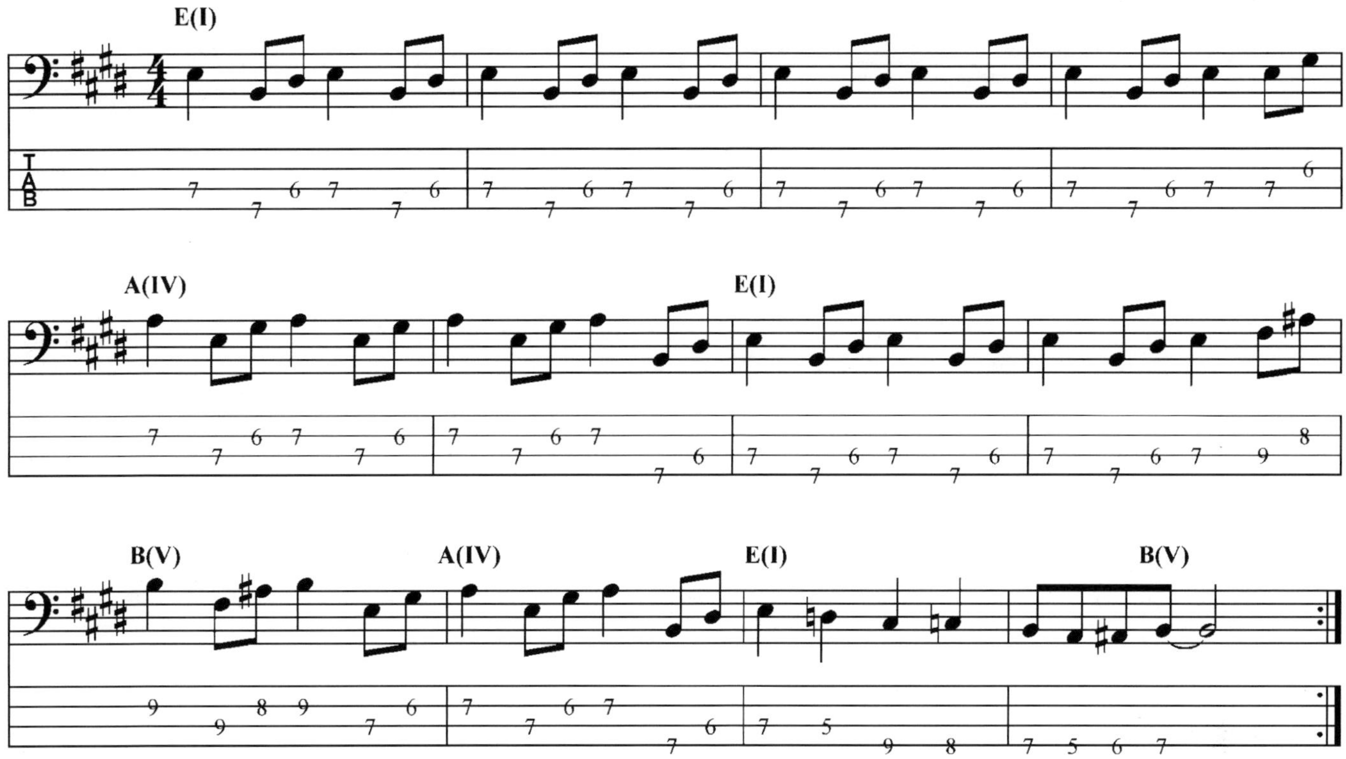

27 This is a Rock Beat, similar to the songs "Nadine" performed by Chuck Berry and "Bama Lama Bama Loo" performed by Little Richard.

28 This is a Rock Beat, similar to the song "Night Train" performed by James Brown.

29 This is a Shuffle, similar to the songs "Nine Below Zero" and "CC Woman" performed by Muddy Waters, as well as "Beepin' On Me" performed by Mark Hummel.

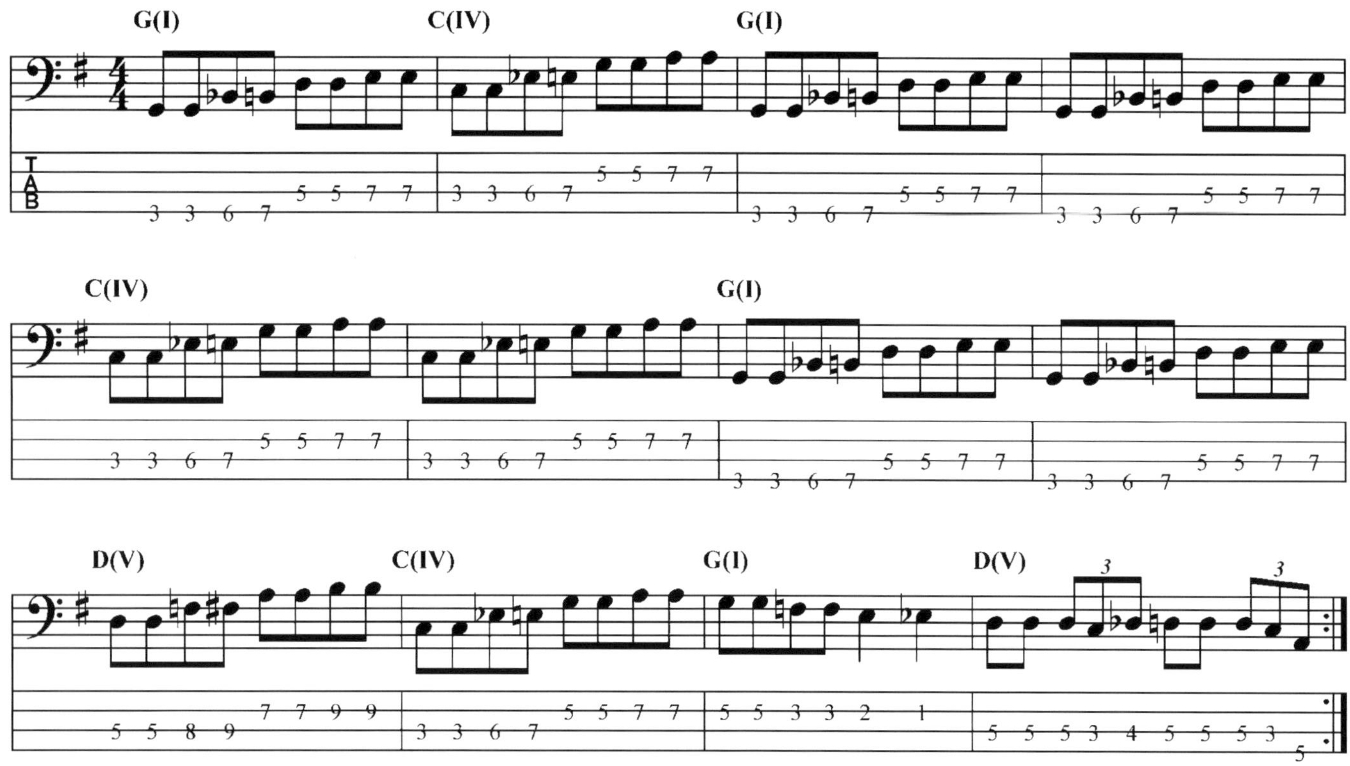

30 This is a Rock Beat, similar to the songs "Lucille" performed by Little Richard and "Just A Little Bit" performed by Johnny Winter.

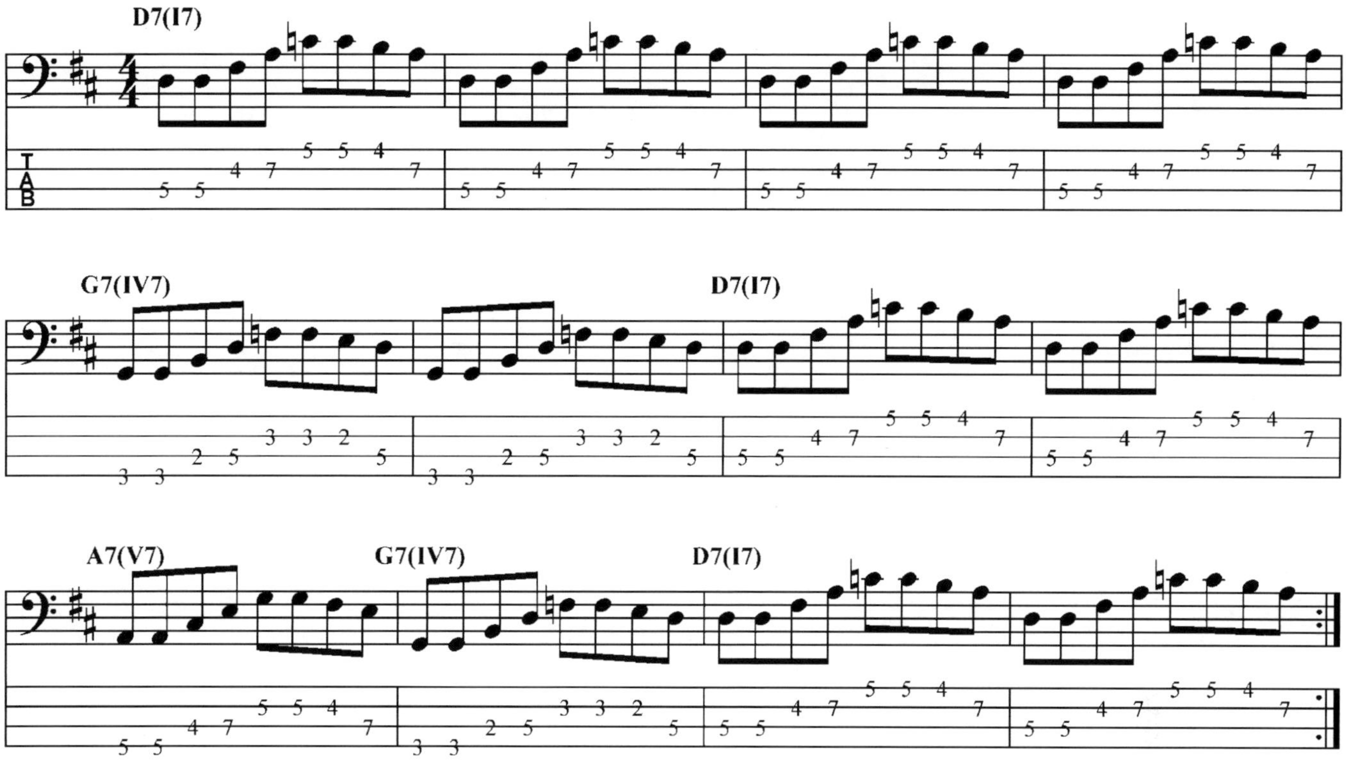

31 This is a Shuffle, similar to the songs "The Feeling Music Brings" performed by Susan Tedeschi and "Greasy Gravy" by William Clarke.

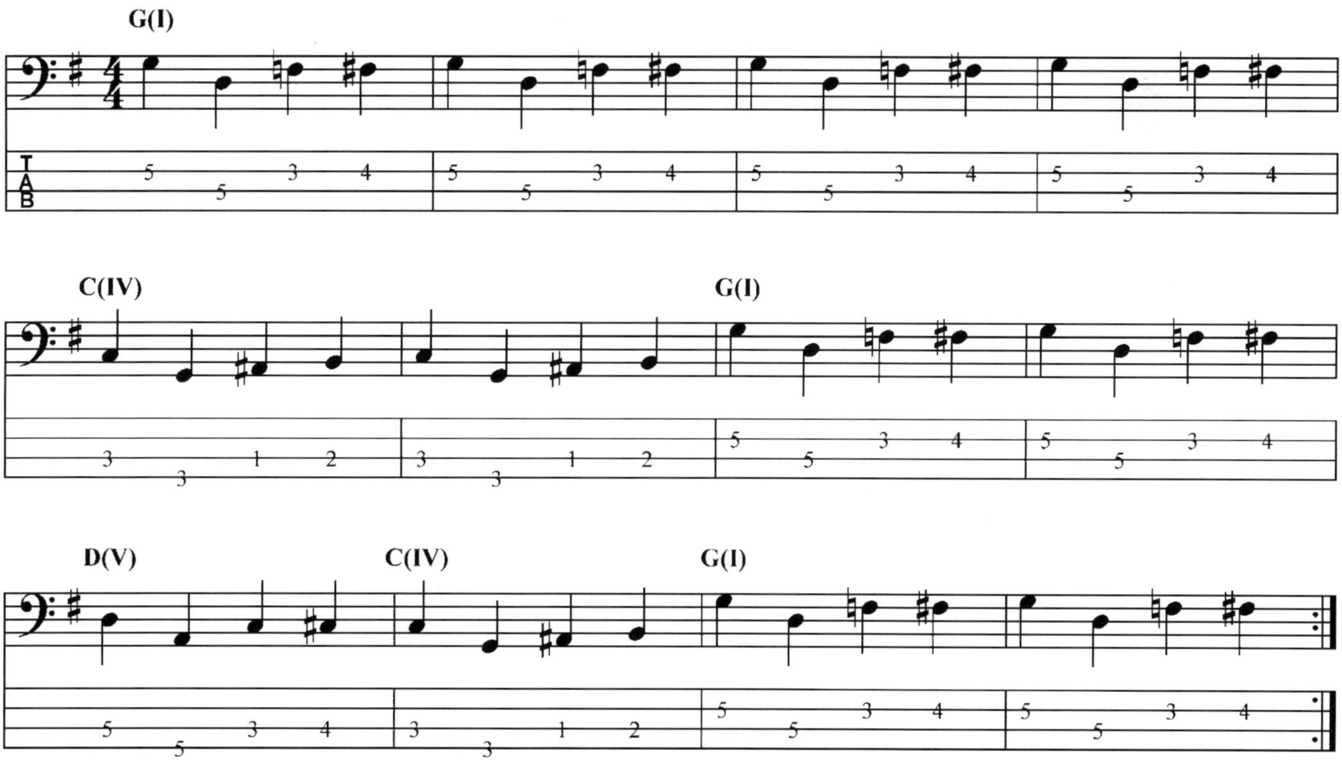

32 This is a Slow Shuffle, similar to the songs "Reconsider Baby" performed by Lowell Fulson and "Laundromat Blues" performed by Albert King.

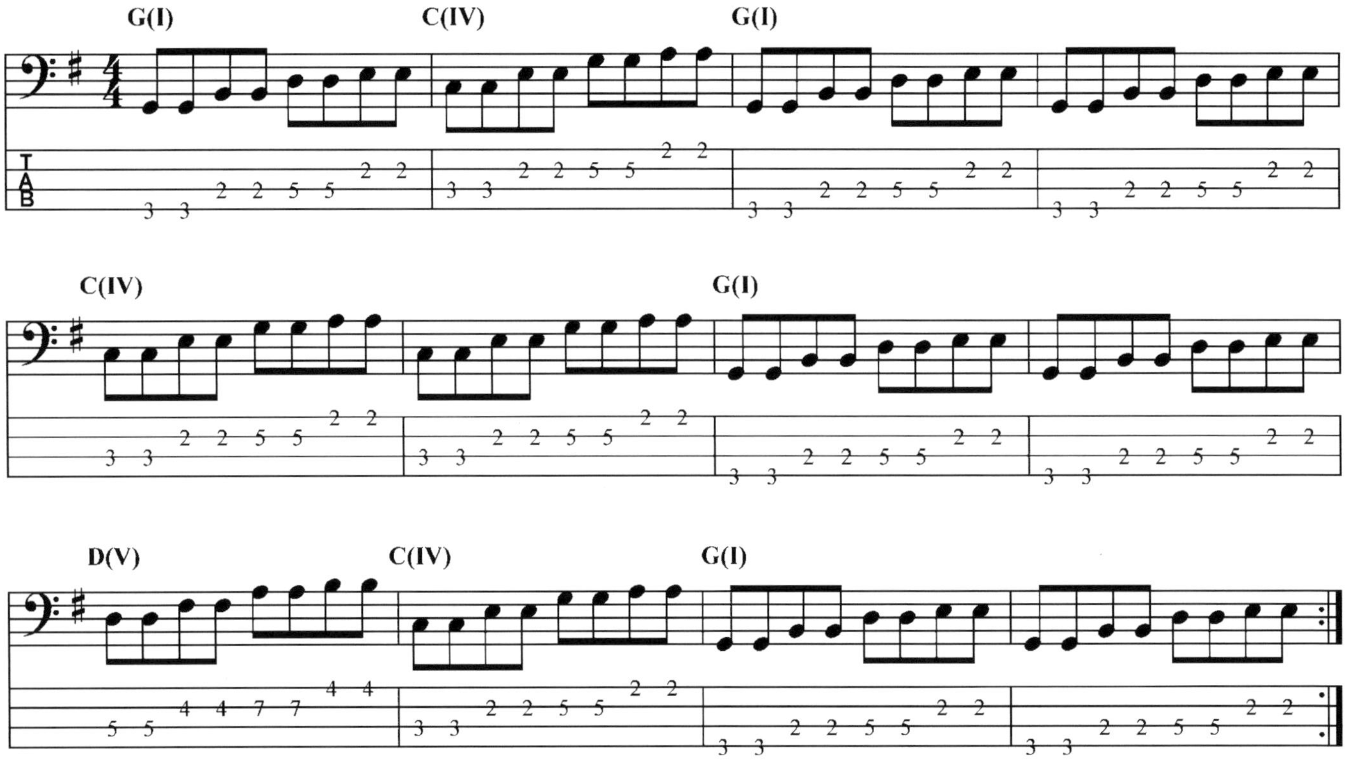

33 This is a Swamp Beat, similar to the song "Baby Scratch My Back" performed by Slim Harpo.

34 This is a slow ballad Blues, similar to the song "Ain't Nobody's Business" performed by Jimmy Witherspoon.

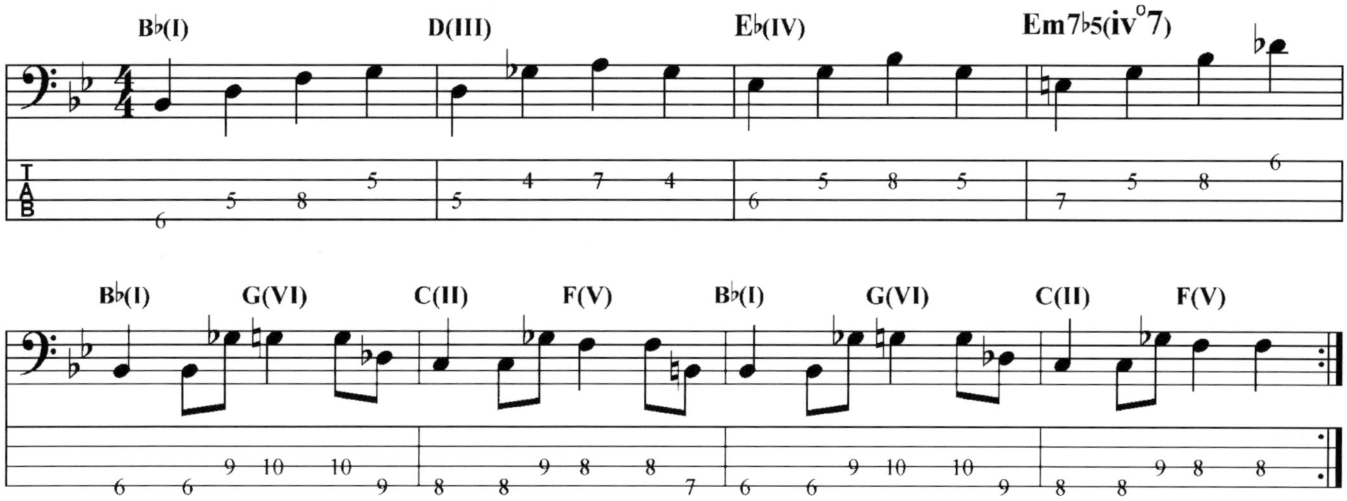

35 This is a Billy Boy Arnold Beat, similar to the songs "I Wish You Would" by Billy Boy Arnold and "Rockinitis" performed by the Hollywood Fats Band.

36 This is a Shuffle, similar to the song "Wang Dang Doodle" performed by Ko Ko Taylor.

37 This is a Rock Beat, similar to the songs "Screamin'" performed by Paul Butterfield and "Cleo's Back" or "Cleo's Mood" performed by Junior Walker & The All Stars.

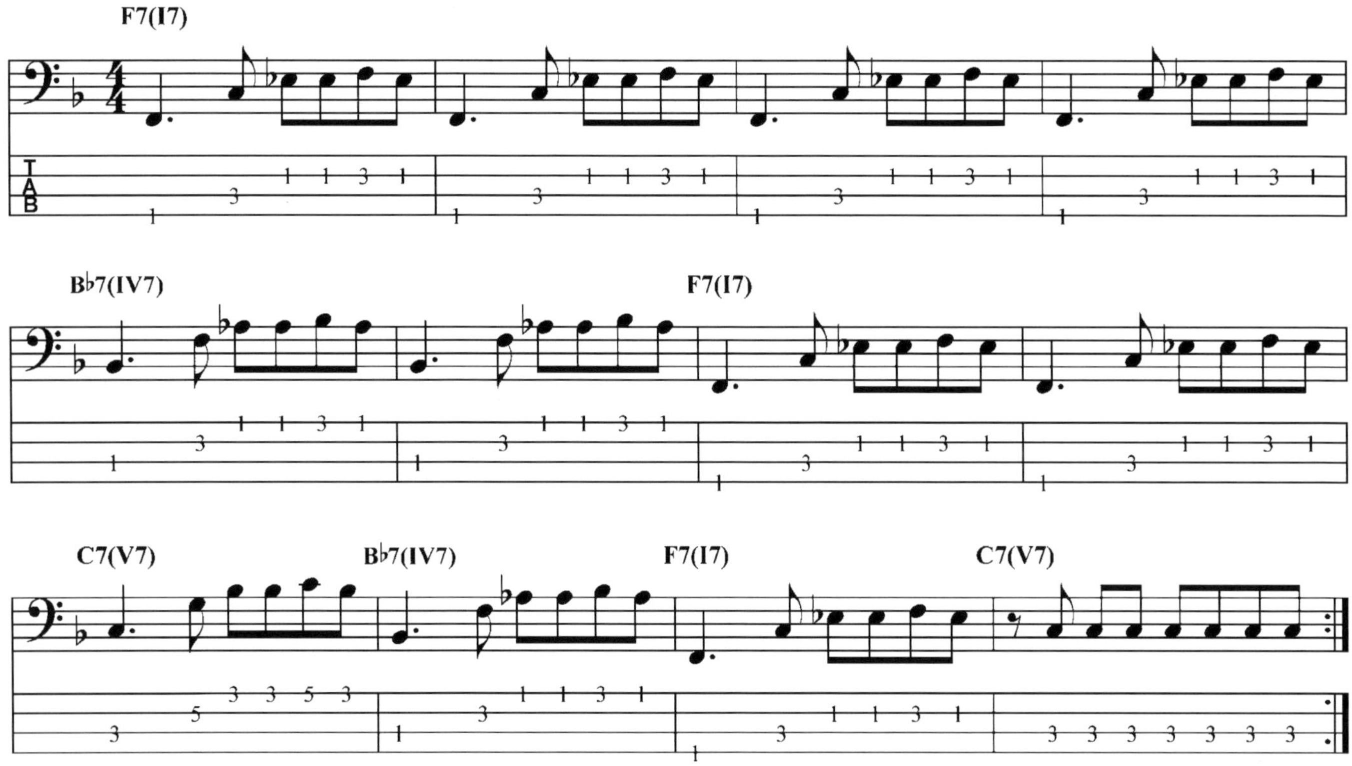

38 This is a Shuffle, similar to the songs "Sloppy Drunk" performed by Jimmy Rogers, as well as "Tell Me Mama" and "It Ain't Right" performed by Little Walter.

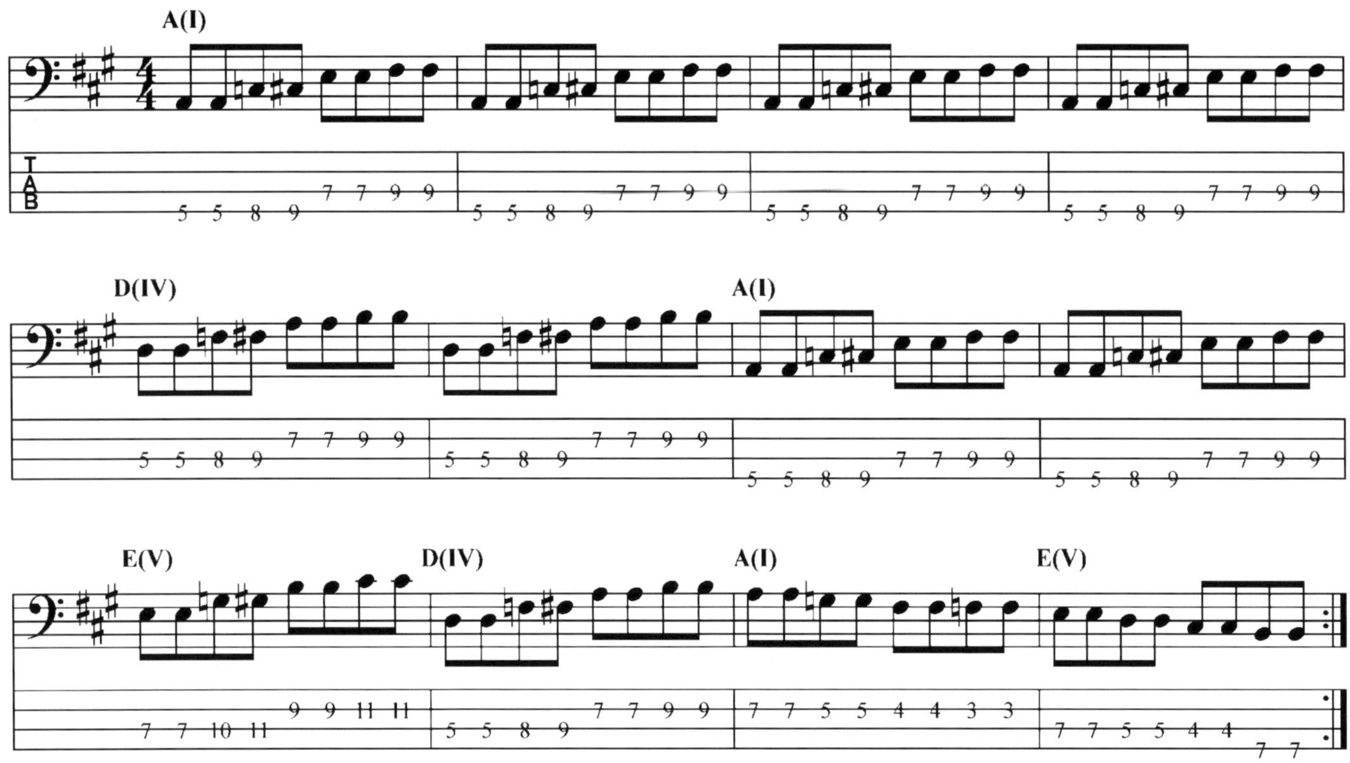

39 This is a Shuffle, similar to the songs "Somebody" performed by Rod Piazza and "Chicago Style" performed by John Garcia.

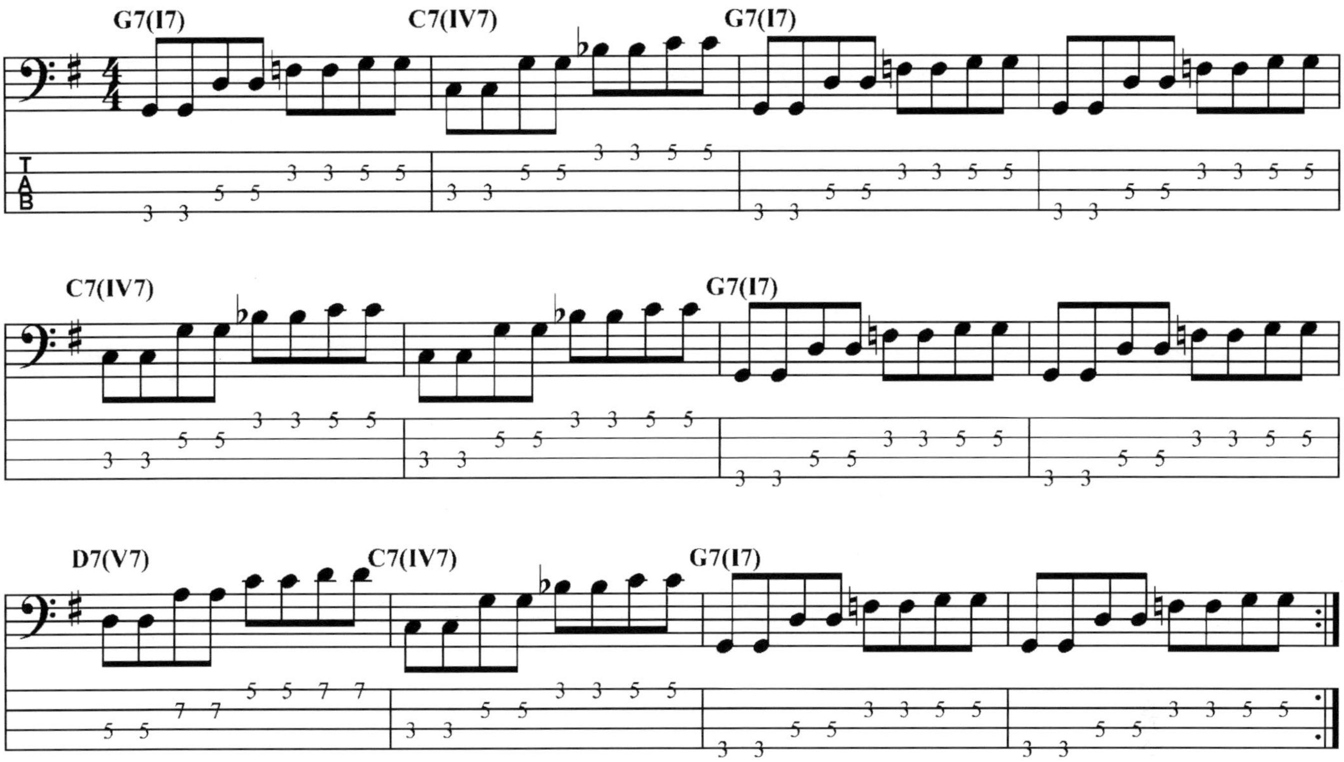

40 This is a Slow Blues, similar to the song "Stormy Monday" performed by Bobby "Blue" Bland.

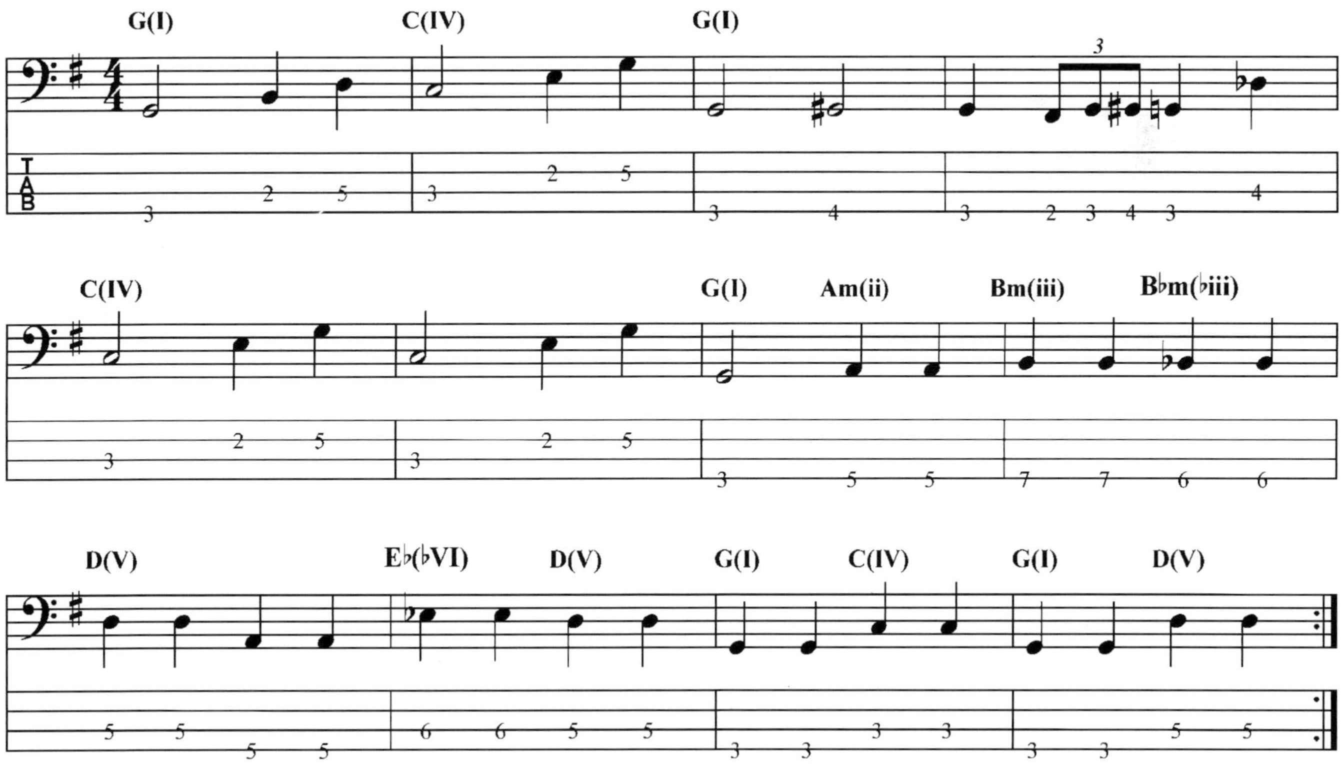

41 This is a Shuffle, similar to the songs "Sweet Home Chicago" performed by Eric Clapton and "Blow Wind Blow" performed by Muddy Waters.

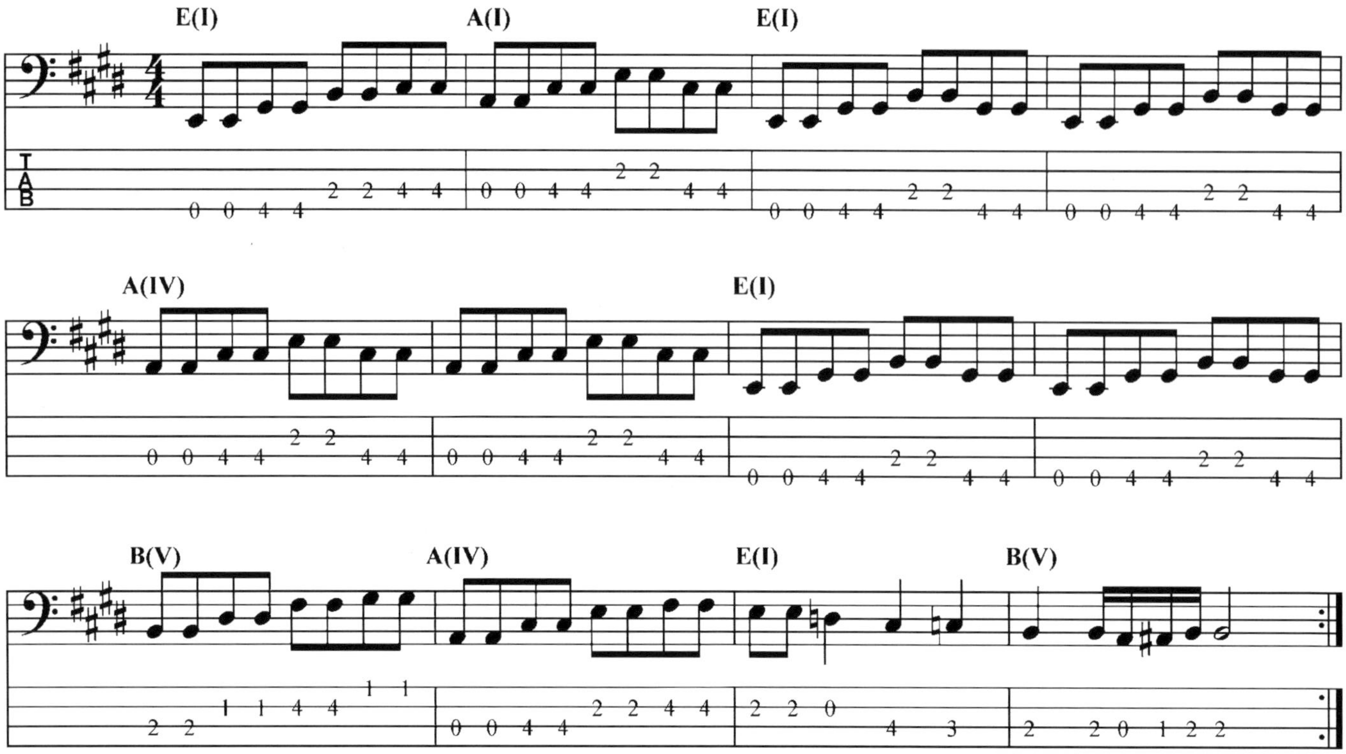

42 This is a Backwards Shuffle, similar to the songs "Tell Me What's The Reason" and "The Hustle Is On" performed by T-Bone Walker.

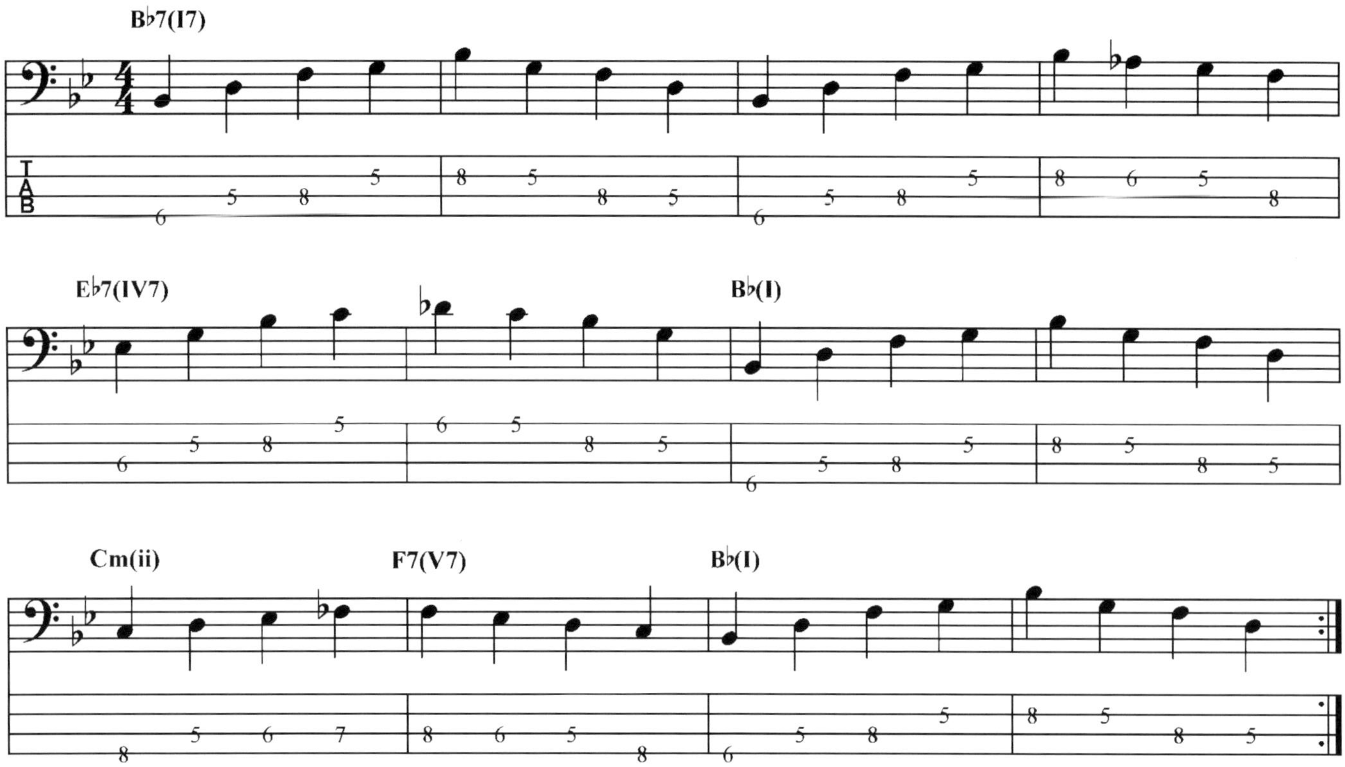

43 This is a Slow Blues, similar to the songs "The Things I Used To Do" performed by Guitar Slim and "If I Should Lose You" performed by Kim Wilson.

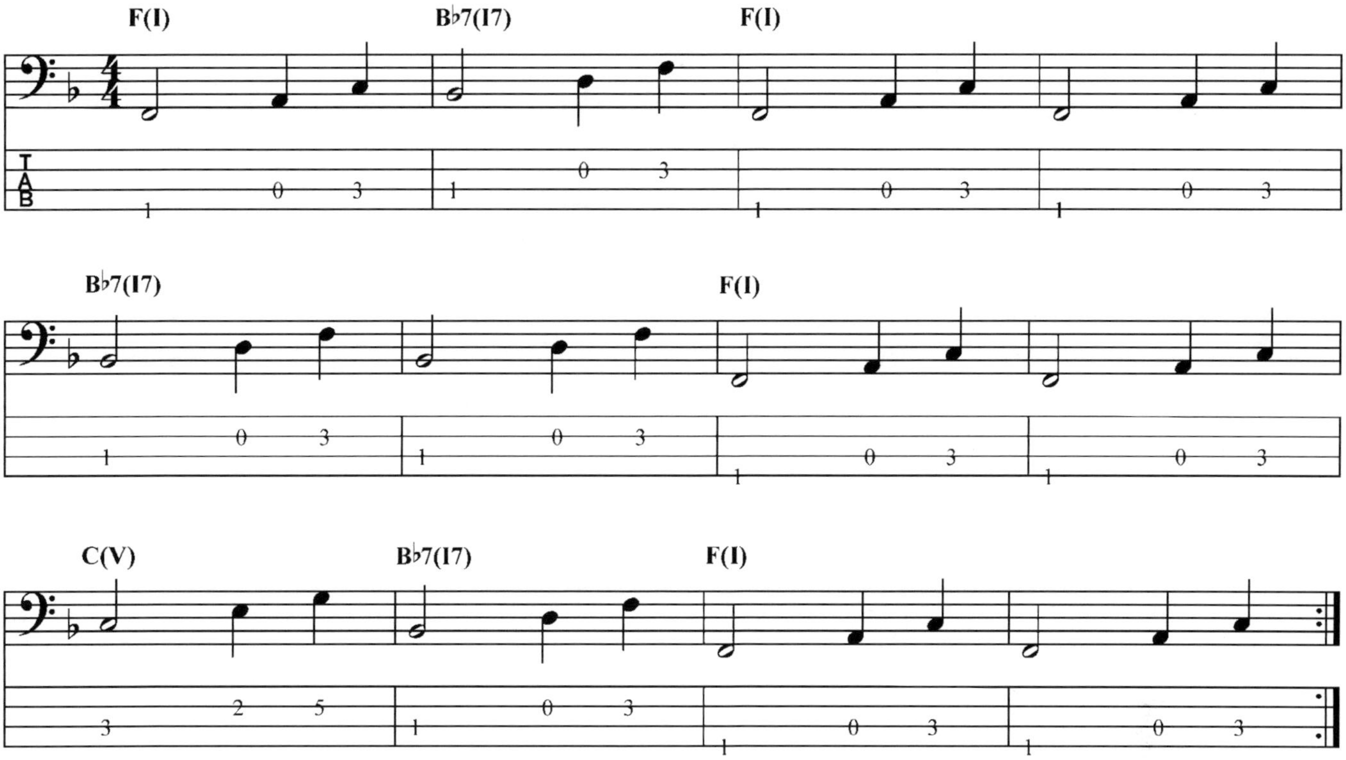

44 This is a Rock Beat, similar to the songs "Tramp" performed by Carla Thomas and "Cash Money" performed by William Clarke.

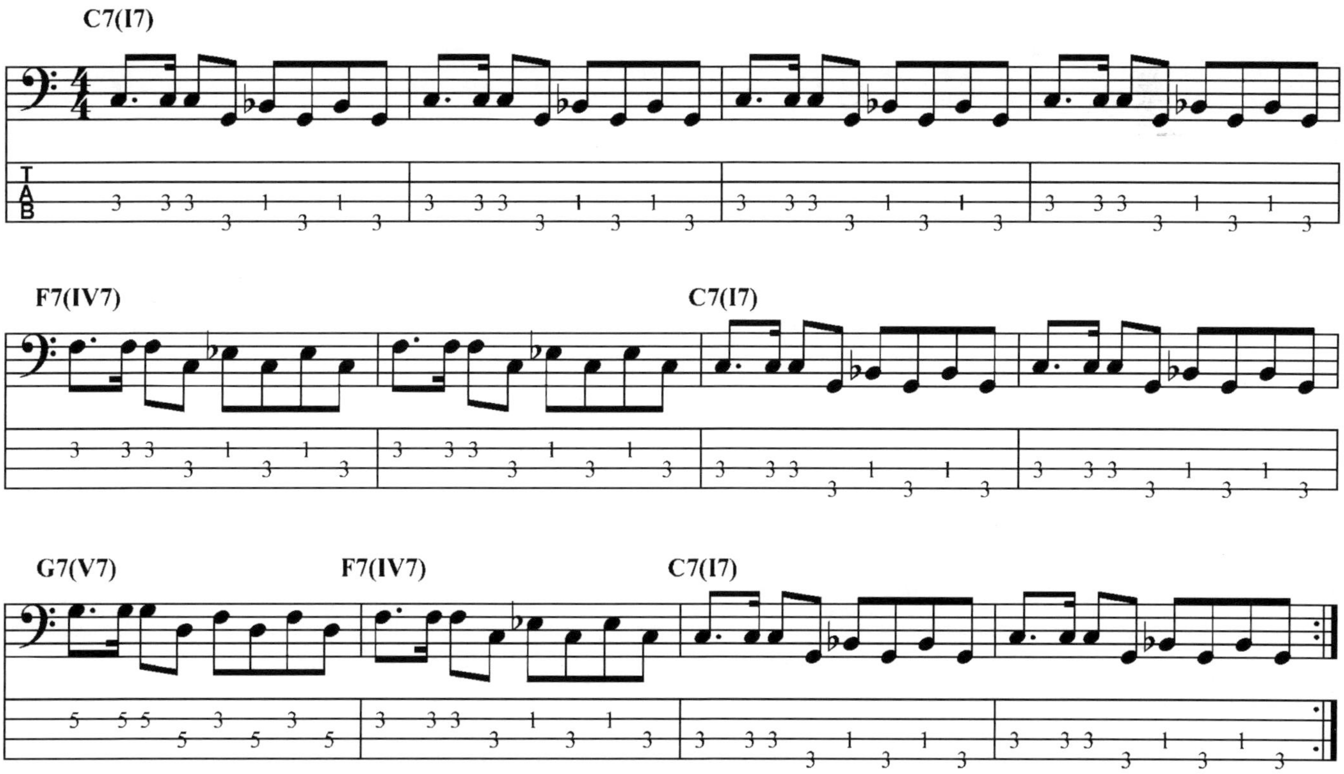

45 This is a Rhumba, similar to the song "Walking To My Baby" performed by Kim Wilson and the Fabulous Thunderbirds.

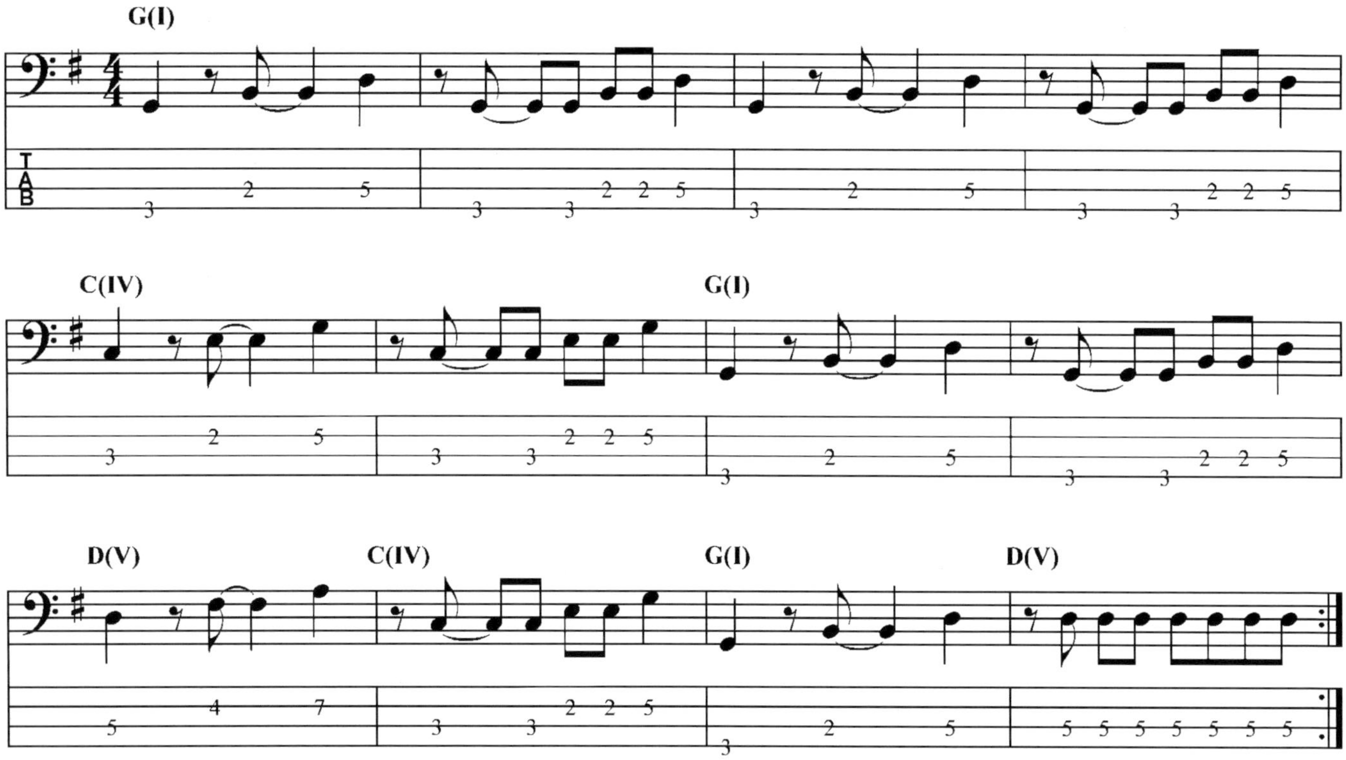

46 This is a Rhumba, similar to the songs "Woke Up This Morning" performed by B.B. King and "Hey Little Girl" performed by Professor Longhair.

47 This is a Stroll, similar to the songs “Rockhouse” performed by Ray Charles and “Walking To New Orleans” performed by Fats Domino.

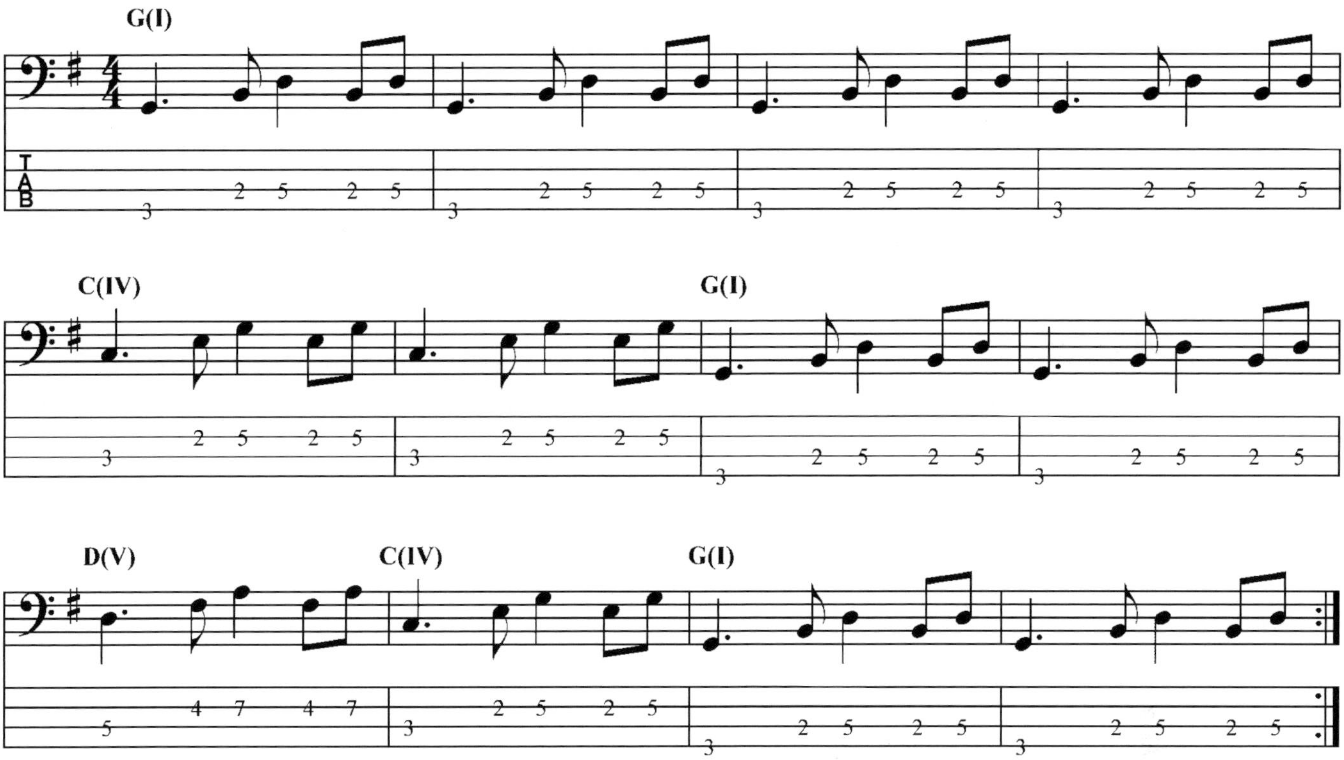

48 This is a Slow Blues, similar to the song “Rock Me Baby” performed by B.B. King.

Final Thoughts

This brings us to the end of our study. It is my sincere hope that I have helped to fuel your passion for learning to play the Blues. If you have enjoyed this book, try my other Mel Bay method books, *Blues Bass Method* (MB21063M) and *Blues Bass Play-Along Trax* (MB21064M).

Recommended Listening

In my private lessons I always stress to my students that they should try to gather a widely varied collection of Blues music. Usually their next question is "Which CDs should I buy?". I've come up with a three-part answer that should help you with this.

First, buy the CDs from the original masters. Artists like Muddy Waters, Little Walter, Willie Dixon, Elmore James, Jimmy Reed, B.B. King, Albert King, Freddie King, James Cotton, Albert Collins, Sonny Boy Williamson II, T-Bone Walker, Paul Butterfield and so on. You can start by purchasing their "greatest hits" albums.

Next, buy CDs from the national touring acts such as Rod Piazza, Kim Wilson, Roomful of Blues, Tommy Castro, Susan Tedeschi, Delbert McClinton, Tab Benoit, Angela Strehli and others.

And finally, buy CDs from the local Blues acts in your region. I have found that local bands produce very good CDs.

This three-pronged approach will give you a very good perspective of Blues music over the last 50 years. You will be able to hear how it has evolved and equally important, how it has stayed the same.

Check our website at www.schooloftheblues.com for information on lessons, workshops and my discography.

School of the Blues Staff

Front Row (L-R): Frank De Rose, John Garcia and Kevin Coggins
Back Row (L-R): Steve Czarnecki and David Barrett

Thanks To...

After more than 40 years of playing music and 30 years of playing the Blues, there are many people to thank that have helped me get to this point in my musical life. First I want to thank the very long list of great Blues musicians that I have played with over the years. Learning about the Blues is a life-long project and every musician that I have played with has contributed to the knowledge that I have acquired to date. I cannot begin to list their names because the list would be far too long for this section of the book. But, there are two key people that I must thank. These are Blues musicians that I have been associated with for 30 years. First and foremost I want to thank Northern California Blues Harmonica Master, Gary Smith. My association with Gary has opened many doors for me in the Blues community and I will be forever grateful for the time that he has spent guiding me during the early stages of my learning about the Blues. Next, I want to thank the great San Francisco Bay Area Blues piano player Sid Morris. The San Francisco Bay Area is home to several great Blues, Boogie Woogie and New Orleans style piano players and Sid is one of them. I have been fortunate to play many years with Sid. These piano styles require the piano player to have a strong left hand (the left hand plays the bass lines) and I have studied his bass lines and learned to play in unison or counterpoint with him. Learning the piano bass lines from these styles of music has contributed greatly to my personal style of bass playing.

Thanks so much to Kevin Coggins, the drum instructor at the School of the Blues. Kevin made significant contributions to this book. He helped by providing suggestions for the types of grooves that should be used in this book. I cannot thank him enough for his research on the subject and his expert playing on these tracks.

Next I want to thank everyone at the School of the Blues. This book would not have been possible without David Barrett and the School of the Blues.

And lastly, I want to thank my wife Peggy and my daughter Bianca for their support and understanding of my endless pursuit of learning about the Blues and playing the Blues.

Credits

- Producer, Editor & Coauthor:
  - David Barrett
- Musicians - The following musicians performed on the recording:
  - John Garcia (Guitar)
  - Frank De Rose (Bass)
  - Kevin Coggins (Drums)
- Band Recording:
  - Soundtek Studios in Campbell, California
  - Engineered by Thom Duell
- Narration Recording:
  - School of the Blues® in San Jose, California
- Context Proof Readers
  - Dennis Carelli
  - John Russell
  - Diane Smith
- Photography:
  - Dave Lepori Photography in San Jose, California